Original title:
The Roots of Reflection

Copyright © 2025 Creative Arts Management OÜ
All rights reserved.

Author: Jude Lancaster
ISBN HARDBACK: 978-1-80566-646-2
ISBN PAPERBACK: 978-1-80566-931-9

Whispers from the Deep

In the ocean's belly, fish wear hats,
Seahorses dance and juggle with bats.
Crabs tell jokes, while bubbles rise,
The starfish giggles, oh, what a surprise!

Waves tickle secrets, under sea foam,
An octopus plays the world's smallest trombone.
Dolphins crack wise, with a flip and a twist,
They swim past the squid, who just can't resist!

Echoes of Forgotten Soil

Atop the hills, a worm wears a tie,
While raindrops fall, making mud pies fly.
The daisies gossip, and daisies prance,
Sipping on dew, they love to dance!

The ants march in sync, a tiny parade,
Critters debate if insects invade.
A beetle's humor is rather absurd,
As it rolls a ball, of what? A turd!

Reflections Beneath the Surface

A pond's mirror laughs, with jokes in the breeze,
    Frogs in tuxedos take turns to tease.
  The water's a stage, for splashes and jumps,
    As turtles snicker at the muddy clumps!

Goldfish in bow ties, swim with such pride,
  Making wisecracks while bubbles collide.
   A lily pads' gossip is rather profound,
  As they float along, never making a sound!

Undercurrents of the Mind

Inside our heads, thoughts twirl and play,
Like rubber duckies that float on a ray.
Ideas bump into each other with glee,
While daydreams wander, sipping iced tea!

Memory hiccups like a clumsy clown,
Wearing mismatched socks and a floppy gown.
Thoughts dance the cha-cha with no sense of grace,
In the circus of brain where we all take our place!

The Heart's Compass

My heart flips like a pancake,
On a Tuesday, for goodness' sake.
Lost in thoughts, a wild gaze,
Like a squirrel in a nutty maze.

I ponder paths, should I go left?
Or chase that pie, like a mad chef?
Heart's a GPS that's lost the plot,
Routing me to the nearest donut shop.

With every beat, it's pure confusion,
Like a cat in a dog's illusion.
Should I dance or should I prance?
Or just sweep in with a clumsy glance?

So here we are, all tangled tight,
Navigating life, full of delight.
If only my heart had better maps,
I'd end up in a land of joyful laps.

Camouflaged Clarity

I looked for wisdom, a sage's face,
But tripped on wisdom's awkward grace.
Shadows dance like socks left alone,
In a drawer of thoughts, forever grown.

I thought I saw truth in a cup,
But it was just tea—messed me up!
The clear path hid behind a bush,
Like a cat whose tail made a loud hush.

Logic wore a disguise, quite sly,
Dressed as a pigeon that learned to fly.
It cooed some facts that swirled around,
But ended up lost, never found.

So here's to truths that like to hide,
In riddles and giggles, they often bide.
Unraveling the funny things I see,
Like a banana peel just waiting for me.

Journeys Within

I ventured deep, a brave explorer,
Inside my head, a bit of a chore-a.
Thoughts were pirates, wild and free,
    Setting sail on a sea of me.

Each corner turned, a bubble bursts,
With treasures found and bloopers first.
A map was drawn in crayon bright,
Leading to snacks I bought last night.

I took a train on the brain express,
    But it derailed, oh what a mess!
Thoughts like trains, they scatter wide,
    Chasing dreams in a humorous ride.

Yet through the chaos, laughter flows,
Each twist and turn, the journey grows.
    In inner lands where giggles glide,
    I'm a captain of this silly ride.

Flickering Echoes of Yesterday

Whispers of yesteryear, so bright,
Like a circus clown hitting the night.
Memories dance in silly hats,
Winking like mischievous spry cats.

Chasing shadows, I trip and trip,
On past adventures, a laugh-filled slip.
Balloons float by, all colors of fun,
Mocking the seriousness of everyone.

I recall the day I said 'hello',
To a tree that waved like it was in a show.
Its branches chuckled, a friendly tease,
While I lost my lunch to a buzzing bee.

Yet each echo brings a smile wide,
Tickling my heart and joy I can't hide.
So here's to laughter in memories tall,
In the carnival of life, we must all fall!

Fraying Threads of Thought

In a tangled mess, my mind does dance,
As socks turn inside out in this wild prance.
I ponder and giggle at the silly fuss,
Why do my notions always play on the bus?

A thought pops up, then takes a quick flight,
I chase it around, but it's out of sight.
Like a squirrel with a nut, I forget what I knew,
Is that my idea, or just yesterday's stew?

Reflections bounce like a rubber ball,
Each glance in the mirror brings laughter's call.
My serious face meets a jester's grin,
It's hard to look wise when your brain's in a spin.

So here's to the threads that unravel my mind,
To the quirks and the giggles, the silly, unlined.
In the tapestry of thought, I find a delight,
For the fraying is fun, and it all feels just right.

The Weight of Fragments

In a cupboard I found a shoe,
Wonder if it's left or right?
With mismatched socks I cannot rue,
Is it day, or is it night?

I collect the bits of my past,
A spoon, a fork, a cat-shaped toy,
Each with a tale that's unsurpassed,
But still they bring me little joy.

My memories all dance a jig,
In a wig, they do the twist,
Each one a silly, quirky gig,
Yet fading fast, they can't persist.

So here I sit with bits and bobs,
Echoes of laughs so divine,
Coping with all these silly jobs,
And hoping for some peace of mind.

Unseen Bonds of Identity

My hat's a bit too big for me,
Yet a crown in my backyard.
I strut like royalty, you see,
With a toaster as my guard.

They say I'm weird, I wear it proud,
With cereal stuck to my face.
In the mirror, I shout out loud,
Just a part of life's big race.

Invisible strings pull and sway,
Family ties in my fruit bowl.
Bananas whisper 'come what may',
While apples plot, oh what a role!

So I dance in my mismatched shoes,
A clown in life's great circus show.
Embracing all these vibrant hues,
As I skip and laugh, and go.

Threads of Yesterday

I found my old remote control,
The one from '93, I think.
Each button holds a tiny role,
Like memories in the drink.

Last night's pizza, a bit too cold,
Became the muse of my daydreams.
In tales of crust, bravery bold,
A hero fought for cheesy themes.

What was that time I wore pink shoes?
Danced in puddles, faced the rain.
My youth a treasure I can't lose,
Yet sometimes feels like a big prank.

So I gather all the silly stuff,
Scraps and laughter in a heap,
Woven threads, though just a puff,
Are memories that I will keep.

Luminous Depths of Memory

A lightbulb flickers overhead,
Has it always been this dim?
I wonder if the snacks I fed,
Could shine like stars from whim.

The fridge whispers in the night,
With secrets of spoiling cheese.
Sweet leftovers, a funny sight,
Like hall of fame for my heart's tease.

A dog with socks upon his paws,
Parades around like he's the king.
While I search for ancient flaws,
In times where giggles gold would sing.

So I gather laughter like confetti,
In messy rooms where life resides.
With weird moments, oh so petty,
Now luminous, where joy abides.

Puzzle Pieces of Existence

In a box with no lid, I find my old socks,
Where logic meets mayhem, and time really talks.
Pieces of laughter, tucked under the fluff,
Mixing up memories, it's all rather tough.

A puzzle so grand, with corners left wild,
I search for the edges, just like a lost child.
Assembling my thoughts, oh what a fine game,
I realize my sanity's never the same.

The pieces keep shifting, a cat on my lap,
With each twist and turn, I plot my next nap.
Existence is funny, like socks in a dryer,
Chasing my thoughts as they dance and fly higher.

In strange orientations, the world spins about,
Finding odd shapes in a jumble of doubt.
With each little giggle, and quickened heart rate,
Confusion's a puzzle and life's just first-rate.

Nimbus of Nostalgia

Oh hail the memories, they rain down like cats,
Sweaters from childhood, and funky old hats.
In clouds of remembrance, I float back in time,
Juggling my yesterdays, a whimsical rhyme.

Azure skies whisper of days lost to haze,
While I trip over facts as I search through life's maze.
Floating on puffy clouds of cake and of cheer,
Each twinkle reminds me of what I hold dear.

The past has a way of donning bright wigs,
Dancing like shadows and prancing like pigs.
In my funny nimbus, I twirl with the breeze,
Dreaming of moments that bring me to knees.

With laughter's sweet echoes, I call them my friends,
Wrapping up time like a gift that just bends.
Together we roam through nostalgia's embrace,
Creating a circus, a most charming space.

Mirror of Moments

I glance in the glass, oh what do I see?
Reflections of chaos just smiling at me.
Moments are juggling, a circus in place,
A funhouse of laughter, oh what a wild space.

With winks and with grins, I wave to my clone,
Each glance pulls a memory right off the bone.
The mirror's a trickster, reflecting my fears,
Yet fills up the room with my whimsical cheers.

Each smirk tells a story, each crack shows a laugh,
A slapdash concoction, a quirky mishmash.
I twist and I turn, chasing what's real,
In the mirage of moments, I dance like a seal.

With every reflection, I find a new tune,
A melody crafting my life like a cartoon.
Oh life's just a merry-go-round in disguise,
Where truth looks back at me, filled with surprise.

Underneath Layers of Thought

Beneath all my layers, what's lurking in there?
I peel back each layer with shrieks and with flair.
Thoughts like an onion, they smell oh-so-strong,
Who knew that my brain would be so very wrong?

Peeking through walls made of funny-shaped dreams,
I uncover each layer, or so it seems.
Balloons, confetti, and jigsaw pieces,
A mix-up of moments that never ceases.

I wander through mazes of tousled ideas,
Stumbling on laughter, tripping on fears.
Each layer I peel is a dance with delight,
In the cake of my mind, I'll spin through the night.

So here's to the chaos, the giggles, the quirks,
Underneath all the layers, my joy now lurks.
I wear it like armor, with sparkles and glee,
In the oddest of thoughts, I finally feel free.

Dreamscapes of the Soul

In dreams that bounce like jelly beans,
We dance with frogs in polka scenes.
A cheese ball sings from up above,
As we chase shadows of our love.

The moon wears glasses and laughs all night,
While owls play poker till morning light.
In this world, all worries cease,
And even the ants enjoy some peace.

With each giggle, the ground does shake,
As silly tunes make the turtles wake.
A pancake flips with quite a flair,
And giggles gallivant without a care.

So let us wander, roam, and sing,
In fields where nonsense is the king.
With dreams that bounce and skip and twirl,
We'll create a wacky, woeful whirl.

Kites in the Wind of Time

Kites dance like chickens on a string,
In the wind, they flop and swing.
They giggle loudly, such a sight,
As clouds giggle back in the light.

Balloons float high, as socks take flight,
They form a band, oh, what a sight!
With every gust, hats fly away,
And rubber ducks join in the play.

Time trips over its own two feet,
While wave-jumping ducks take a seat.
As giggly breezes flip our hair,
The kites and laughter fill the air.

So let's soar high, release our mind,
Forget the worries we must bind.
In this strange dance where whimsy's prime,
We'll chase the kites through winds of time.

The Canvas of Thoughts

Paint splatters like a confetti storm,
Colors collide in a wild form.
Brushes tap dance on the floor,
As ideas shout, 'We're here for more!'

A cat in pajamas holds a parade,
While socks conspire to make a trade.
Thoughts twist and twirl, all in a mix,
Creating a circus of silly tricks.

The canvas giggles, it cannot lie,
It captures all the dreams that fly.
With laughter, we sketch out our fears,
And smear them away with joyful sneers.

So grab a brush and let's create,
A masterpiece of dreams that wait.
In this crazy art-filled dome,
We'll laugh and paint ourselves a home.

Breaths of Self-Discovery

Taking breaths that sound like giggles,
We trip on thoughts and do the wiggles.
With each inhale, a chuckle stirs,
And every exhale flings out furs.

We search for sense in a shoe parade,
Where thoughts and ducks waddle, unafraid.
In a garden of whimsy, ideas sprout,
Each bloom a riddle, twist, and shout.

Silly voices fill the air,
As we dance with socks without a care.
In every breath, a joke takes flight,
Laughter echoes in the twilight.

So discover selves with whimsy bold,
And let your stories brightly unfold.
With every laugh, your spirit flies,
Creating joy beneath the skies.

Subterranean Thoughts

Deep below in muddy gloom,
Where worms and worries spin and zoom,
I ponder life, a tangled vine,
With jokes that twist and roots that twine.

A gopher grins with mischief bright,
Saying, 'Dig deep, it'll be all right!'
The dirtier the thought, the funnier it seems,
As I laugh with mice and questionable dreams.

What if rocks all had a say?
They'd gossip like the stars at play!
In caverns dark, where echoes chase,
A ticklish feeling finds its place.

So down I go, with humor intact,
To mine the jokes, it's a curious fact!
And in this soil, I find my cheer,
With worms that wriggle and tickle my ear.

The Weaving of Ancestors

In a loom of laughter, threads unwind,
Grandma's antics come to mind,
With needles sharp and puns so thick,
She knit a smile that's bound to stick.

Old Uncle Joe, with stories grand,
Tells tales of toads and a 'fishing hand,'
Each stitch a giggle, woven tight,
At family gatherings, such pure delight!

Cousins tumble, tangled in yarn,
A fabric of follies, a colorful charm,
With every knot, a memory blooms,
As laughter echoes through the rooms.

So gather 'round, while we weave anew,
With threads of joy, and maybe stew,
For all the quirks that make us whole,
In the tapestry of our family soul.

Beneath the Waves of Time

In ocean depths where fish all prance,
Time swims by in a silly dance,
A dolphin laughs and flips its tail,
While jellyfish joke and set the scale.

Seashells whisper of moments past,
Where crabs play cards, their luck unsurpassed,
With every wave that rolls on high,
Comes laughter darting 'neath the skyline.

Old boot, a treasure, stirs a laugh,
It tells of sailing, a noble craft,
As barnacles snicker on a rock,
Counting the hours on the tick-tock.

So let's dive deep where humor flows,
In tides of wit, the world just glows,
Beneath the surface, smiles abound,
In currents of laughter, joy is found.

Hidden Currents of Being

Beneath the surface, giggles hide,
In currents strong, they twist and glide,
A fish with glasses swims right by,
Saying, 'Life's better when you laugh and try!'

The riverbanks, with their quirky view,
Whisper wisecracks, old and new,
As frogs croak jokes that split the air,
Each splash a punchline, hiding somewhere.

What if rocks could tell your tale?
They'd chuckle softly, never stale,
In hidden depths, where shadows play,
A comedy club, where laughs convey.

So paddle forth on the waves of glee,
For the world is a joke waiting to be,
A current flowing, merry and bright,
In hidden laughs, we find our light.

Echoing Silence of the Past

Back in time, I dropped my watch,
It bounced and rolled, a grand old clutch.
I chased it down through muck and grime,
Reflecting on my sense of time.

The echoes here, they giggle loud,
As memories dance, so unbowed.
A squirrel mocks, with cheeky glee,
While I discuss my flaw with me.

I ponder what the stones have seen,
In whispers soft, it feels routine.
But really now, they just sit tight,
Heavy stones don't join the fight.

So take a step, hear what they say,
It's just my mind, who wants to play.
With laughter steeped in ancient lore,
I find the past a real big bore!

Traces of Light Through Canopy

Sun beams dance like little sprites,
Peeking through the leafy heights.
They tickle leaves, they tease the ground,
In nature's games, joy's always found.

I squint and grin, scratching my head,
What do these beams wish to spread?
A light that's cheeky, bright, and bold,
A prankster's tale that's yet untold.

The trees above, they shake and sway,
In laughter shared, they play the day.
I ask them for their secret plan,
But all I get's a wise old 'bran'.

So through the trees, the fun resides,
As shadows dance and laughter hides.
For if you look, you'll find your view,
Canopy giggles, giggling too!

The Veins of Old Stories

In every line, a story flows,
Tales of squirrels and noses, who knows?
Each knot and twist, a sketchy past,
Makes me feel, 'Gee whiz! This won't last!'

Old tales swirl beneath the bark,
They whisper secrets, leaving a mark.
But by the end, I find I'm lost,
In squirrel gossip that counts the cost.

Each twist and vein, a winding ride,
Where laughter pops and feelings glide.
If only trees could share a drink,
What juicy tales would they all think?

So here I sit, a curious sage,
With roots that wobble with every page.
Read the bark? Or walk away?
Guess I'll stick around for another day!

Mirrored by the Earth

The ground reflects my silly face,
A mirrored fun, a funny place.
I strike a pose, the soil grins wide,
And giggles ripple, like a tide.

I make a leap, I twist my feet,
The earth responds, it can't be beat.
It chuckles back with all its might,
"Oh please, just help me, you take flight!"

Each step I take, a bounce, a smile,
The earth and I, we chat awhile.
In muddy shoes, my style defined,
With laughter shared, our hearts aligned.

So leap I shall, and spin around,
For mirrors echo jovial sound.
And as I dance, a joyful birth,
I find delight mirrored by earth!

Spiral of Discovery

In the depths of my mind, I dive,
Finding thoughts that wiggle and jive.
One looks like a taco, the other a shoe,
I should not be hungry when searching, it's true.

My ideas are clearly a colorful mess,
They dance like they're wearing a bright polka dress.
I thought I found wisdom, but all that I gained,
Was a recipe for fruitcake — frankly, I'm pained.

The rabbit I chased was a hole in my brain,
With laughter it zipped, leaving me in vain.
In spirals I whirl, chasing thoughts that might fit,
But all that I find is the noise of a bit.

So here's to the journey, the giggles we find,
In the wild chaos of what's tangled and twined.
With every odd thought that tickles my brain,
I laugh and I cheer, it's all part of the game.

The Silence Between Words

Between the thoughts, silence sneaks,
Whispering secrets that tickle our cheeks.
It's in the pauses, the beats of our chat,
Where strange little creatures sneak out — fancy that!

A hiccup, a snort, more than a pause,
The quiet can cause laughter without any cause.
Like when my cat sneezed, and I burst out in cheer,
It had nothing to do but made sense somehow here.

In the gaps, I imagine a dance with no feet,
Where squirrels make speeches and owls bring the beat.
A wise old crow caws in tones oh so clear,
While I ponder the meaning of sour versus beer.

So hold onto silence, it's full of surprises,
With giggles and chuckles in all shapes and sizes.
Between every word, in each giggling quake,
Lies laughter and joy, for goodness' sake!

Echoes of Yesterday

In the attic of memories, echoes do play,
Like a cat in a hat that is lost in the fray.
I found an old photo where I struck a pose,
With spaghetti for hair and a nose made of toes.

Yesterday's laughter bounces around,
Like a pogo stick bouncing and making a sound.
I recall the bright shirt that made my mom fret,
As I danced with a cucumber — a sight hard to forget!

The echoes remind me of silly old jams,
Where I sang to the goldfish, and danced with the hams.
A symphony made of giggles and grins,
Each note a reminder of all of my sins.

So here's to the yesterdays, wild and absurd,
With all of their stories, nonsensical words.
In every old echo, a chuckle I seek,
A journey through laughter, so wacky and unique.

Voices in the Stillness

When silence hangs like a banner so bright,
Voices emerge doing impressions of flight.
A sock on the floor thinks it's making a call,
While the fridge hums tunes like a rockstar at hall.

In the quiet, the toaster starts telling its tale,
Of bread that was caught in a jam with a snail.
The clock ticks in rhythm, a metronome tease,
As the laughter of teapots floats up on the breeze.

A brush with a mop keeps the floor in its care,
While a broom whispers secrets of dust in the air.
Each object a comedian, bright and quite silly,
Turning stillness to giggles, oh my, what a willy!

So next time you sit in a room that is bare,
Listen closely, for voices are dancing with flair.
In the stillness they twirl, in a delightful parade,
Embracing the nonsense in which we've all played.

Secret Pathways of the Heart

In the garden of thoughts, where giggles grow,
A squirrel once danced in a hat made of snow.
With each playful twirl, he chased his own tail,
While pondering life over a mug of stale ale.

Behind every smile, there's a wisecrack or two,
Like a clown at the circus, he slipped on a shoe.
Chasing the shadows of wisdom so sly,
He chuckled at clouds that just wouldn't comply.

A flower once asked, "Why do bees like me so?"
The answer, oh dear, was a buzz full of woe.
Yet beneath all the laughter, the truth takes its part,
In the secretive pathways that waltz through the heart.

So let's toast to the quirks that we often neglect,
Like socks missing mates and the things we forget.
For life is a joke with a punchline so clear,
A riddle of joy in the laughter we share.

Flickers of Awareness

In the corners of mind where the dust bunnies play,
A thought popped up like a dog on the way.
With a wag of its tail and a curious bark,
It chased after shadows that danced in the dark.

Awareness tickled like feathers on skin,
As I tried to recall where I'd put all my pins.
Each flicker a flame, oh what could it mean?
A light bulb above that just needed some gleam.

Like a lamp in the attic that flickers with glee,
Or a cat on a windowsill, watching the spree.
Awareness so playful, it hops and it skips,
As it teases the mind with its joyful quips.

So here's to the moments we stop and we stare,
When a sneeze makes us jump and we can't help but swear.
In the dance of an eyelash, a giggle, a spark,
The world comes alive in the light and the dark.

Patterns of the Past

In the fabric of time, where old habits lay,
A sock puppet dreams of a glorious day.
It reminisces of yarns spun with laughter and grace,
And the times it was worn as a goofball in space.

Patterns emerge like the wrinkles on skin,
A quilt made of memories packed deep within.
With each stitch a story, a laugh, or a tear,
The fabric of life often leads us to cheer.

The past is a trickster, with jokes up its sleeve,
It plays hide and seek while we try to believe.
That behind every fumble, a lesson will bloom,
Like a flower adorned in a grand living room.

So let's wear our patterns, our polka dots proud,
Dance like the peacocks, sing loud, be unbowed.
In the humorous tales that our memories cast,
We find precious gems in the patterns of past.

Musings Beneath the Boughs

Beneath branches heavy, where whispers take flight,
A squirrel sips tea with the moon every night.
They plot little schemes to confuse the wise owl,
Who rolls his great eyes at the fur and the growl.

The boughs are the stage for a comedy skit,
With acorns as props and the sun as the wit.
The breeze brings applause, rustling leaves like a crowd,
As laughter erupts in the shade, warm and loud.

A grasshopper jokes that he's got perfect hops,
While a turtle feels proud, saying, "Slowly, it tops!"
Underneath the old oak, where silliness reigns,
The heart finds a rhythm, and joy breaks the chains.

So let us all gather in this playful refuge,
And dance like the fireflies, spreading our huge
Giggles and grins through the dappled light beams,
In the musings beneath where laughter redeems.

Tangles of Understanding

In logic's maze, we often jest,
A puzzle piece that won't find rest.
Twisted thoughts like spaghetti strands,
Who knew wisdom needed rubber bands?

With questions bouncing like a ball,
Answers hiding, hear their call.
An avalanche of witty charms,
Straightened paths lead to alarm!

Through missteps, laughter echoes clear,
Reality's twists bring joy and cheer.
We dance around life's silly pranks,
Pondering mistakes while passing flanks.

In each confusion, humor's found,
As knowledge slips and tumbles 'round.
So let's embrace our tangled states,
While we question all of fate's debates.

Submerged Landscapes

In puddles deep, we take a dive,
Where thoughts swim by like fish alive.
The current pulls, we laugh and splash,
Understanding's mud, a funny mash.

With every wave, we float and glide,
Silly fish, nowhere to hide.
Our ideas drift on buoyant dreams,
Finding wisdom in wobbly seams.

Fishy wisdom strikes again,
As coral jokes dance in the fen.
Beneath the surface, muck and mire,
Where giggles bubble with desire.

So take a plunge, don't fear the sea,
Let's paddle through absurdity.
For in the depths of laughter's song,
We might discover we belong.

Lanterns in the Dark

With lanterns lit, we roam around,
In shadows deep, our laughs abound.
Glowing bright, the jokes take flight,
Guiding us through the quirky night.

In dark corners, whispers gleam,
Silly secrets, like a dream.
The flickering light of half-baked plans,
Keeps us joking, hand in hands.

Each shadow dances, plays a trick,
Chasing us with a playful flick.
But in the glow, we start to see,
The humor that sets our minds free.

So here we are, with lanterns bold,
Sharing stories that never get old.
Through the dark, our laughter shines,
Brightening paths with twisty lines.

Veils of Reflection

Behind the veil, the fun unfolds,
Where thoughts wear masks, the mystery molds.
Clownish faces in mirrored grace,
Each glance reveals a silly place.

With every peek, a giggle springs,
Reflections dancing, wearing rings.
Our wits like mirrors, clash and gleam,
Creating a most comical theme.

In layers thick, we laugh a lot,
Through funny slips and a tangled plot.
Tell me your secrets, behind that screen,
I'll share mine too, in this whimsical scene.

So lift the veil, let laughter reign,
In this carnival of joy, no need for pain.
For in such mirth, we find our truth,
Hidden behind every comical sleuth.

Mosaic of the Mind

Pieces scatter, thoughts collide,
In this jigsaw, we can't hide.
Puzzles placed without a clue,
Is that a rabbit or just my shoe?

Colors clash with lively glee,
A masterpiece of wackiness, see!
Fractured memories tag along,
Singing out a silly song.

Traces of Time

Tick-tock, my clock's a tease,
It runs amok, just like a breeze.
Yesterday's here, tomorrow, who cares?
Lost in a haze of mismatched pairs.

Worn out shoes from days gone by,
Chasing shadows, oh me, oh my!
Each step a dance, a wobbly glee,
Do we grow old, or just feel free?

Ripples in the Waters of Self

Splashing thoughts in a mirror's wave,
Reflecting back, oh, how we rave!
Witty echoes, a hearty laugh,
Is that wisdom or just a gaffe?

Wiggle, wiggle, the reflections play,
Who knew deep thoughts could be so gay?
A whirlpool forms, then calms the storm,
In the shallow end, absurdity's norm.

Chasing the Inner Light

A flicker found beneath the mess,
What's that? A light? Or just my dress?
With flashlights on, we run around,
In pursuit of clarity, but what's that sound?

Chasing beams that jump and jive,
Who knew a glow could feel so alive?
Tripping on thoughts, we giggle and sigh,
Is enlightenment near, or am I just shy?

Echoing Silhouettes

In the mirror, I see a grin,
A funny face wearing a chin,
Oh, how it laughs at my wild hair,
Not a style, but a clumsy affair.

Shadows dance as I strike a pose,
One foot here, but the other doze,
Twisting and turning, I create a sight,
Who knew reflections could bring delight?

Giggling echoes fill the room,
As my silhouette takes on gloom,
Pretending to be a star on stage,
Oh, the funny things we engage!

With every twist, I find the groove,
The more I sway, the more I move,
Laughter reverberates all around,
In shadows, my joy is truly found.

Threads of Connection

With a needle and thread, I try to sew,
Some wisdom that's hard to bestow,
A tangled web of thoughts I weave,
Oh, the stories my brain can conceive!

Sewing buttons of laughter in place,
Mixing ideas with a quirky grace,
I thread my shoes but they won't tie,
Why do all funny mishaps comply?

Pulling at strings of giggles and snickers,
As the fabric of life gets thicker,
I patch a smile here, patch a joke there,
Life's a quilt, and I'm unaware!

In my sewing circle, it's quite a blend,
With laughs and snorts, this chaos transcends,
Gathering threads, all colors span,
Together we stitch a comedic plan.

The Soul's Mosaic

Pieces scattered, some bright, some dim,
A jigsaw puzzle, looks quite grim,
I try to fit them, but oh what fun,
Each crazy piece makes me want to run!

With every tile, a story unfolds,
A duck in a hat? The art it holds,
Mixed emotions, one goofy dance,
Searching for sense in this wild romance!

Underneath the chaos, joy does shine,
I see my flaws as a sparkling line,
Crafting a picture, wonky and great,
In this mosaic, I celebrate fate!

A smile here and a giggle there,
Crafting a soul with tender care,
Imperfect beauty dances in tow,
In every shard, my laughter will grow.

Insights in Petals

A flower blooms, it winks and laughs,
Hiding secrets in its colorful halves,
Petals flutter, whispering tales,
With bees that dance like silly quails!

I stop to smell all the floral cheer,
In each sweet scent, joy appears,
The daisies giggle, the roses tease,
Oh, how nature's humor brings me ease!

With every petal, wisdom's revealed,
Trust in the zany, let it be sealed,
Nature knows how to make us chuckle,
In insightful petals, we find our huddle!

Dancing with flowers, what a delight,
Life can be goofy, but oh so bright,
In gardens of laughter, we grow and sway,
In the petals' embrace, we find our way.

The Garden of Thought

In the garden where ideas bloom,
Thoughts sprout like flowers in a room.
But some weeds grow tall and wide,
Tickling minds, they can't hide.

The bees buzz with questions, oh so sweet,
While ants march with lines on repeat.
Sunflowers nod like they know it all,
But daisies just giggle and start to sprawl.

Each thought a veggie on a shelf,
Slice of humor served by oneself.
Lettuce laugh at what we find,
In this garden, we're all inclined.

Tides of Introspection

Waves of thought crash and retreat,
Surfing memories in flip-flop feet.
Seagulls squawk with wisdom's glee,
As crabs dance in a philosophy spree.

The tide rolls in with questions wacky,
About socks forgotten and laundry tacky.
Casting nets for pearls or pies?
Just fishy tales whispering lies.

Oh, how we paddle back and forth,
Seeking treasure of quirky worth.
Kites fly high with ideas bold,
Yet land makes us do as we're told.

Underneath the Surface

Beneath the water, fish debate,
What's on the menu, mate or fate?
Turtles joke about their slow pace,
While eels zip by, a slick embrace.

Coral castles hold secrets tight,
As clownfish dance in delight.
The seaweed whispers funny quotes,
While sharks take selfies with their votes.

Bubbles carry tales of fishy dreams,
Fluffing up laughter in goofy streams.
It's a fin-tastic life under here,
Where giggles swim with a little cheer.

Veins of Solitude

In silence, roots stretch far and wide,
Tickling thoughts wherever they reside.
A tree in the dark wearing a tight grin,
Confusing the critters that peek within.

Squirrels chat about the acorn lore,
While shadows play hide and seek at the core.
A breeze whispers secrets, oh so sly,
But leaves just chuckle as they wave goodbye.

In this solitude, the fun's a blast,
While branches sway like they're having a laugh.
Deep in the earth, roots tangle and tease,
As life giggles softly with the trees.

Serpentine Paths of Insight

In a garden of thoughts, I wander and whirl,
Chasing down bubbles that dance, twirl, and swirl.
But alas! They pop, and I'm left with a grin,
The wisdom in giggles, where nonsense begins.

I ponder the ants with their grand little plans,
Marching in circles, or forming a dance.
I ask them for guidance, they just stare at me,
Their tiny brains working on tea and a spree.

The sky tells me secrets with clouds in a row,
Each shape a riddle, a whimsical show.
I see a potato, then suddenly—chicken!
It's hard to find wisdom when laughter's so lickin'.

So here I shall sit with my tea and my mind,
Let the cosmos confound while the laughter unwinds.
For in paths of confusion, I'll learn to delight,
In the joy of the journey, I'll dance through the night.

The Mirage of Time's Embrace

In the clock's ticking dance, oh what a surprise,
Time plays peek-a-boo with its mischievous eyes.
I ask for a minute, it giggles and flies,
A jester in shadows, with laughter it ties.

Each moment a mirage, I reach but it slips,
Slipping like ice cream on sweet, silly trips.
I swear it's a trick, a grandiose jest,
Time's hiding behind, creating a quest.

I ponder the seconds, they chase like a hound,
Barking for me to get up from the ground.
They tug at my sleeves, while I'm stuck in my chair,
A merry-go-round of absurdity rare.

So I laugh at the whims of this time that's so coy,
A riddle wrapped tightly in giggles and joy.
For each tick is a reason to dance and to play,
Making moments of nonsense the best sort of sway.

When Nature Speaks Within

The trees are chatting, with whispers so sly,
A rustling of leaves, a wit they supply.
"Why so serious, friend? Drop your worries and frown!"
They sway and they swirl, with their leafy gown.

Birds tweet upon branches, like nature's own choir,
Creating new lyrics that soar ever higher.
I try to sing back, but I sound like a frog,
They chuckle and chirp, "Just embrace the fog!"

The flowers gossip in a vibrant bloom,
Sharing their secrets while banishing gloom.
With petals so colorful, they plot and they plan,
To tickle the air in a sweet garden span.

So here in the laughter of nature's own crew,
I find myself giggling at each silly view.
For when all's said and done, and I've danced my own way,
Nature's punchline brings joy that is here to stay.

Remnants of Forgotten Journeys

In the attic of memory, dust bunnies gleam,
Whispers of journeys both silly and dream.
I stumble on treasures—my old socks with holes,
They clap at my feet, like excited moles.

Maps spread like laundry, a quest to the moon,
With markers for pizza, and dates for cartoon.
I squint at the scribbles, my compass all wrong,
Finding my way through the laughter, a song.

These relics remind me of roads less than clear,
Of socks on my hands, juggling cars and a deer.
Each trip a grand jest, a folly-filled spree,
With echoes of giggles and charming mishap glee.

So I salute the odd paths that laughter unveils,
Those remnants of journeys where fun never fails.
In the chaos of memories, I find my own way,
With socks by my side, I'll conquer the day!

The Dance of Silent Roots.

In the garden where snails twirl,
The worms do twister, and squirrels swirl.
Fungus giggles, tickling the earth,
While mushrooms boast of their hidden mirth.

Grasshoppers leap, in tune with the ground,
Their dance is silent, but oh, what a sound!
They twiddle their antennas, in perfect unison,
As ants carry crumbs, in their great fusion.

Beneath the daisies, the laughter erupts,
While sunflower heads nod, as if they've corrupted.
Petunias gossip of secrets they got,
The secrets of veggies, just steaming in pots.

So join the fun, don't be aloof,
Earth's silent party is quite the goof!
With roots underground, the laughter goes deep,
Next time you stomp, take a moment to peep.

Beneath the Silent Surface

Bubbles pop beneath the pond,
Frogs debate how to respond.
Tadpoles giggle, in tiny suits,
Arguing who has the best swimming boots.

The fish wear glasses, quite out of place,
While lily pads join in the race.
Dragonflies cheer with wild delight,
For under the water, the fun's out of sight.

Old turtles roll their weary eyes,
As they witness all the silly highs.
The water's calm, but chaos brews,
With laughter echoing, as if on cues.

So if you dip, don't make a fuss,
Join the soiree, it's all a plus!
With every splash, a joke does flow,
Beneath the surface, the jesters glow.

Echoes of Forgotten Dreams

In the attic where dust bunnies play,
Old toys grumble of yesterday.
Forgotten dreams in a toy box piled,
Whispered stories, ever so wild.

A soldier sews, while a doll pretends,
To patch up the seams of imaginary friends.
Teddy bears snicker, their bellies round,
As they reminisce on the mischief found.

Paper airplanes take flight with glee,
Stir up the shadows, so carefree.
Old records spin with a scratchy tune,
While the clock ticks gently, a soft monsoon.

So listen close to the echoes of cheer,
In the attic's corners, where dreams persevere.
With giggles and grumbles, they softly beam,
A whimsical world from forgotten dreams.

Whispers in the Mirror

In the mirror where secrets collide,
Reflections giggle and take a glide.
Noses twist, and faces morph,
Creating portraits of ludicrous worth.

A wink here, a pout there,
Each glance reveals a joyful affair.
The hair flips with a feathery grace,
Making odd shapes in a charming race.

Lipstick mischief, a wild spree,
The countenance dances, oh so free.
Brushes tickle, and mascara sneezes,
While laughter erupts in twinkling breezes.

So next time you step to take a look,
Remember the whispers in every nook.
For within the mirror, stories explode,
A comedy show on a bright abode.

Layers of Knowing

In a garden full of thoughts so bright,
I stumbled on a worm in flight.
It wiggled and jiggled, a funny sight,
Telling secrets through the night.

Buried deep beneath the soil,
Ideas grow with little toil.
Each layer laughs and has a hoot,
Imagination in a rooty suit.

What if dreams sprout legs and run?
Chasing laughter, oh what fun!
The more I dig, the more I find,
Worms wearing hats, oh so kind!

So let's unearth what lies below,
With every giggle, watch it grow.
In layers thick, we'll share a joke,
With wisdom wrapped in mirthful smoke.

Fractions of Infinity

If time could split like a pizza slice,
I'd count the toppings, oh so nice.
A sprinkle here, a laugh from there,
Eternity's tickles are quite rare.

I ponder on my half-sliced day,
With fractions floating in a fray.
The more I try to make it whole,
The less I grasp that silly goal.

Counting moments that fly so high,
Adding laughter like pie in the sky.
A piece for you and one for me,
In infinite jest, we'll always be free.

So grab a fork, let's eat our time,
In this bizarre, poetic rhyme.
With every bite, a chuckle's cheer,
Infinity tastes like chocolate beer!

Veins of Experience

In the heartbeat of a quirky tree,
Branches tell of you and me.
With every knot, a tale unfolds,
Of laughter shared and adventures bold.

Through leaf-blown wisps, I hear the jokes,
From ancient bark to silly folks.
The winds whisper secrets, oh so grand,
As squirrels debate who's the funniest in the land.

Each vein carries thrills, a twist of fate,
Where mischief blooms and smiles create.
Tickling roots and dancing twigs,
All join in for the laugh that digs.

So let's climb high where the giggles grow,
On branches soft, with friends in tow.
With every bounce and playful tease,
We'll write our stories in the breeze.

Dreaming in Colors

In a canvas where the wild things play,
I dip my brush in the colors of play.
With giggles painted in bright neon,
I craft a world where wackiness is drawn.

The sky's a splash of raspberry swirl,
While zebras tiptoe and twirl.
Clouds giggle in fluffy white,
As rainbows dance like it's a night.

Each hue whispers a silly tune,
Here, even shadows wear balloons.
Every brushstroke is a hearty laugh,
As squirrels host a pie-eating gaffe.

So let's paint the dreams we adore,
In colors that make our spirits soar.
With every stroke, we find delight,
Creating joy from morning till night!

Memory's Tapestry Unraveled

In the attic, a sweater so bright,
Worn by Uncle Joe, what a sight!
It clashed with his pants, a real joke,
Was he colorblind? Or just poking fun, folks?

Photos with smiles, oh so wide,
But look closely, folks, there's some pride.
Grandma's feathered hat, so tough to wear,
She danced like a chicken; we couldn't help stare!

A time capsule bursting with laughter and cheer,
Mom's epic hairdo, like a bird, my dear.
Dad's weird glasses, with lenses so thick,
We put them on, and we all feel a kick!

So here's to our past, with its quirks and charms,
We stumble and giggle, in its warm arms.
Each moment a thread in this tapestry bright,
Woven together, our memories take flight!

Seeds of Contemplation

In a garden where silliness sprouts,
A gnome on a throne, you would doubt!
With a smile so wide, and a hat so tall,
He whispers secrets of veggies to all.

Carrots with sunglasses, tomatoes with flair,
Zucchinis in shorts dancing without a care,
The radishes giggle, the herbs do a jig,
While the pumpkins just sit, looking big!

A seed of a thought, how deep it can grow,
From thoughts that are silly to dreams that overflow.
We laugh at each sprout, at each funny face,
In this patch of thoughts, we all find our place.

Oh, what a bounty, of smiles and jest,
Where each little bloom feels truly blessed.
So let's plant our dreams in this garden of fun,
And see what reflects when the day is done!

Shadows in Still Water

By the pond where the frogs sing,
There's a turtle that's wearing a bling.
He dives below with a splash so loud,
As the fish all giggle, it draws a crowd.

Reflections of clouds that dance and sway,
But watch out! That duck just stole my play!
With a quack and a flap, he's off in a flash,
But in his wake, the ripples clash.

The cattails whisper secrets untold,
Of frogs in tuxedos all brave and bold.
Each shadow a tale in the warm sunlight,
As laughter ripples, an amusing sight!

So come take a peek at this watery world,
Where shadows of antics are playfully unfurled.
With giggles and splashes, we let out a shout,
In nature's reflection, let silliness sprout!

Beneath the Bark: A Silent Story

In the heart of the woods, there lives a tree,
Whose face looks puzzled, poor dear, oh gee!
It wears all the carvings from kids who would play,
A heart, a "Mom," and a chicken ballet!

Squirrels take note of this wooden art piece,
While raccoons discuss if these marks they increase.
"Did you see that one?" "I thought it was grand!"
"A craftsman's delight, made with a band!"

Under the bark, so much laughter lies,
Where critters exchange the best of wisecries.
Each knot tells a tale of ruckus and fun,
As the seasons come by, their stories are spun.

So here's to the trees, so full of surprise,
With laughter that echoes from roots to the skies.
Each scribble a reminder, so silly, so free,
Of the joy we can find, beneath bark and glee!

Yearnings of the Heart

When love was just a single glance,
I thought I'd find my soulmate's dance.
But then I tripped on my own shoelace,
And landed in a funny place.

I wrote a note, so sweet and bright,
But slipped it in the wrong outfit's sight.
Now every time they wear that shirt,
I feel my heart just twist and hurt.

With every fast and fleeting sigh,
My heart, it seems, can never fly.
It's stuck below those awkward vibes,
Amidst the jokes, the laughter thrives.

But through the blunders, truth will show,
That laughter's love can often grow.
So let's embrace this silly art,
And dance our way into the heart.

Footprints on Forgotten Paths

I wandered down a twisty road,
Where memories hide in laughter's load.
Each step I took, a funny slip,
Reminded me of friendship's trip.

We played hide-and-seek with time,
Wore silly hats, it felt just prime.
But yards away, I felt a thud,
It's just my past, it fell with a 'bud.'

The footprints left were quite absurd,
One showed a dance; one flapped like birds.
With markers bold, they'd scream and shout,
'You've lost your way, but not your clout!'

Yet every scratch upon this ground,
Is filled with giggles all around.
So let's re-trace with joyful plots,
And laugh at all those silly thoughts.

Labyrinths of Memory

In mazes where old tales reside,
I took a turn and then I cried.
For every corner held a jest,
That popped me right out of my chest.

With paths that twist like spaghetti,
I lost my train, felt oh so petty.
A joke from years, it made me grin,
While chasing down where I have been.

The walls they whispered things so wise,
Yet I still cringed at my surprise.
For all those moments, locked in jest,
I'd navigate, they'd be my quest.

Through laughter, I will find the key,
To navigate that wobbly sea.
With giggles, I'll unlock each door,
And trip back down that memory floor.

Wings of Past

I took to skies with wings so bright,
Flew high on dreams, what a sight!
But gusts of memories took me low,
As I dodged the 'oops' from long ago.

Mishaps carried on feathered flaps,
I swooped to miss in awkward laps.
Laughter echoed 'neath the sun,
While chasing clouds, I thought it fun.

Every turn brought tales to tell,
Of silly slips and close to fell.
Yet from the heights, I learned to glide,
Cackling loud, with joy inside.

So here's to flight, that won't go flat,
With knots of joy, where we're all at.
In every flap, there's humor found,
As winds of past keep spinning 'round.

Roots of Future

I planted seeds with dreamy flair,
But who knew trees would grow in air?
A twisty trunk, a comical sight,
And branches sprout with all their might.

I thought of futures, bright and grand,
Yet found I'd grown a sock-shaped brand.
A tangle here, a chuckle there,
This silly fate was quite unfair.

Yet roots beneath still giggle low,
For laughter's course does help us grow.
From knotted dreams, a twisty line,
That leads to joy, a light divine.

So here I stand, with sprouts so bright,
And plant a hope, with laughter's light.
For every root, it plays a part,
In this ridiculous, funny art.

The Inner Echo Chamber

In a room that's filled with chatter,
I heard my thoughts all start to splatter.
They bounced around with quite a flair,
And left me grinning like a bear.

With echoes loud and giggles spry,
My brain's a fairground, oh me, oh my!
Each silly thought, a bouncing ball,
Who knew my mind could be this tall?

I shouted out a joke or two,
And heard them back as something new.
What's this, a pun? A clever jest?
My inner voice, the stand-up guest!

So here I sit in this delight,
Where crazy thoughts take flight at night.
Next time I ponder, I just may,
Invite my echoes out to play!

Streams of Insight

In a river where ideas flow,
I dip my toes; what's this? Oh no!
A fish of wisdom jumps on by,
With scales so bright, I want to cry!

I splash around, I seek to reel,
A catch of thoughts; I'm on a meal.
But every time I think I win,
The fish just turns – and back again!

With little ripples of surprise,
They splash and giggle, oh how they rise!
A stream of quirks with every splash,
These crazy thoughts make quite the hash!

So if you seek a thought to find,
Just grab a net, and clear your mind.
For in this stream, the best jest waits,
With fishing lines and silly fates!

Vines of Wisdom

Tangled vines with lessons bold,
I climb aboard; their tales unfold.
They twist and twine in playful dance,
Each leaf a chance for a silly prance!

One vine whispers, 'Watch your head!'
While another laughs and says, 'Just tread!'
I swing and sway, a forest clown,
With wisdom's jester's floppy crown!

Grapes of thought hang ripe and round,
I gather them, the best I've found.
But as I munch, the juice slips free,
And stains my shirt like a comedy!

So heed the vines and take your chance,
For wisdom loves to laugh and dance.
With every twist and silly flick,
You'll find that humor's quite the trick!

The Hidden Forest

In a forest where the shadows play,
I found a tree that's on holiday.
It swayed and laughed, a goofy sight,
With branches that tickled the moonlight.

A squirrel with glasses, looked so wise,
Told me stories of surprise.
Each acorn dropped was like a gig,
Turning my thoughts into a jig!

The leaves would chuckle, the grass would sing,
As laughter echoed through the spring.
In this realm, a joke took flight,
Where even trees get a bit of fright!

So if you're lost in thought or jest,
Seek out this forest, it's the best!
With funny friends both small and tall,
You'll find the laughter, after all!

Shadows of Inner Landscapes

In gardens where my thoughts do roam,
I tripped on weeds, found my lost comb.
The daisies giggled, the tulips blushed,
As I serenaded them, they merely hushed.

I spoke to clouds, they rolled their eyes,
'No rain for you,' they said with sighs.
The sun peeked in, threw shade on my woes,
While grasshoppers laughed at my fashion faux pas.

A squirrel held court on a branch up high,
He judged my dancing, I wondered why.
Yet still I swayed, full of glee,
While acorns dropped like confetti on me.

So I'll stroll through these shadows with my silly hat,
Each thought a butterfly, imagine that!
With every step in my wobbly shoes,
This inner landscape gives me the blues... but who'd refuse?

Fragments of Stillness

In a quiet room where silence sings,
I found my thoughts on rubber bands with springs.
They bounced around in a playful race,
And tripped over dust in an awkward chase.

The lamp chuckled as it flickered low,
'You're lost in thought, yet here we go!'
I offered it tea, but it preferred to hum,
While I sat thinking, 'Oops, I forgot the crumbs!'

Reflection mirrors showed my socked feet,
Couch crumbs and cushions made quite the seat.
I pondered deeply on yesterday's pie,
While my pet goldfish grinned, 'Give it a try!'

In fragments of stillness, thoughts do collide,
I dance with my shadows, take them for a ride.
With laughter echoing in the empty room,
I wonder if silence could sell me a broom.

Branches of Memory

In the tree of life, memories swing,
Some wear the crown like a catchy ring.
While others dangle, somewhat out of reach,
Telling tales of time, as if they teach.

A branch creaked loudly, it begged for a break,
'You're not my fruit!', said the berry-smoked cake.
Memories tangled like spaghetti strands,
I laughed at the thought—oh, how time demands!

A squirrel flipped backward, a daring display,
Chased by a shadow that wanted to play.
I tried to remember the number of times,
I slipped on banana peels with silly rhymes.

Oh, branches of memory, swing me around,
Keep me from falling, just don't let me drown.
In this canopy of laughter, I'll stay and explore,
With every wobble, I'll ask for some more!

Depths of Contemplation

In the depths of thought, where ideas dive,
I found a whale wearing a bow tie alive.
He winked and said, 'Life's a curious game,'
I chuckled at shadows that danced without shame.

The octopus scribbled with its ink-filled flair,
As I floated along in my old, worn chair.
Each tentacle waved like a wild band leader,
Playing sweet tunes with no need to be sweeter.

Fish flipped acrobatics, they laughed with delight,
'Can contemplating help you to write?'
I pondered the answer while twirling my pen,
What if fish taught wisdom now and again?

So in these depths where the currents run free,
I'll don my snorkeling gear, come swim with me.
With giggles and laughter, let's swim out of sight,
In contemplation today, I'll be a silly delight.

Portraits of the Self

In mirrors, my face shows a grin,
With eyebrows raised, let's begin.
I joke with my shadow, it rolls its eyes,
Saying, "We both know you're full of lies!"

A selfie taken, I strike a pose,
But my hair's doing what nobody knows.
My outfit's a clash, like socks with sandals,
They say fashion's art, I say it's vandal!

Reflections can be a perfect jest,
When I wear a clown nose, I'm at my best.
The laugh lines deepen with every joke,
And my heart feels light beneath the cloak.

So here's to portraits that catch our quirks,
In the gallery of life, nobody lurks.
Each funny echo feels like a song,
In mirrors of laughter, we all belong.

The Hidden Whisper

In quiet corners, secrets abide,
With giggles hiding as they confide.
A sneeze from the cat makes us all jump,
Among these whispers, my heart starts to thump.

My thoughts are like squirrels that dart 'round the bend,
Chasing each other, will they ever mend?
I wear socks that occasionally clash,
And giggle so hard I might just crash!

The walls have ears, or so they say,
Listening closely, but they won't play.
I tell them my jokes, they just stare back,
Maybe bricks don't appreciate my knack!

Hidden whispers, in giggles they bloom,
Shadows dance laughing, filling the room.
In silence, we find the funniest cheer,
So let's toast to laughter, let's hold it dear!

Depths Unexplored

In depths where my sock drawer does lie,
A sweater from '99 waves goodbye.
I dive for treasures, what do I find?
A sandwich from lunch… now that's unrefined!

With goggles on, I enter my mind,
Searching for gems of a peculiar kind.
Is that a laugh or just a loud snore?
Could be a thought, but I'm unsure anymore!

Exploring the depths, I stumble on jokes,
In the whirlpool of nonsense, laughter evokes.
Like fish that can't swim, we flop with delight,
In this vast ocean, everything feels right!

So let's laugh at adventures, lost yet adored,
Between silly shuffles and cakes over-sugared.
In the depths unexplored, we twirl and we spin,
Collecting our chuckles—let's dive right in!

Patterns in the Stillness

In quiet moments, the silliness thrives,
Like cats with wigs, oh how it jives!
A dance with a teapot, a waltz with a chair,
Patterns emerge from the thoughts in the air.

We sit in stillness, a grand masquerade,
Where socks on our hands become the parade.
With hats made of fruit, we muse about life,
In this stillness, there's joy amid strife!

Observing the dust, how it twirls in the sun,
Each speck is a dancer, oh, what fun!
We giggle at shadows that sway and impress,
In quiet dimensions, we'll never digress.

So here's to the patterns that laughter can weave,
In stillness so funny, we truly believe.
Let's cherish the moments, the whimsy we find,
In the dance of existence, we choose to be kind!

The Reflection's Embrace

In the mirror, I dance and sway,
But my hair has chosen to stray.
It twists and twirls with glee,
A spectacle, just for me!

My reflection winks, oh what a tease,
So I twirl back, with the greatest of ease.
Is that a smile or a grimace?
With these antics, I'm a preposterous case!

Jellybeans bopping on my head,
Did I eat too much, or is it just dread?
Each jiggle brings a giggle loud,
As I play solo for my invisible crowd!

A flicker here, a ripple there,
My fidgety self—oh, how it's rare!
Reflecting in my bubble of fun,
With my goofy dance, the giggles are won!

The Unseen Tapestry

Weaving dreams I won't unravel,
Through line and thread, I start to travel.
Swirls of nonsense, colors bright,
A fabric that giggles at night!

I stitch in secrets, snickers galore,
Each tug and pull opens new doors.
A patch of laughter, a thread of cheer,
Who knew my sewing could bring such sneers?

In the tapestry, a raccoon prances,
With socks on its paws, it takes its chances.
Unraveled, I laugh till I can't stand,
For all stitched together is quite unplanned!

A fabric so silly, it drapes and flops,
Catching the eye, as humor hops.
The unseen joy in every seam,
In this woven wonder, I live the dream!

Nature's Quiet Confessions

Upon the branch, a squirrel sneezes,
Echoes through forest, nature pleases.
A hiccup here, a flap of wings,
Each blunder makes the woodland sing.

The river whispers secrets low,
While frogs in their croaks steal the show.
A turtle slips, it's quite a scene,
Nature's funnies are always keen!

The flower giggles in sunlit hue,
As bees buzz by, in quite a flue.
Petals twirl with joyful might,
A silent chuckle, what a sight!

In amusing whispers, they confide,
Secrets shared, rolling with pride.
Nature's laughter, soft yet grand,
In the folds of silence, it's perfectly planned!

Reverb of the Inner Echo

In the caverns of my mind, it bounces,
Hilarious thoughts with giggles it trounces.
A thought about cake goes round and round,
Oops, that echo's got me spellbound!

Dancing ideas pop like balloons,
Each one a jest, sung to silly tunes.
A chuckle here, a snicker there,
Who knew my mind could throw such flair?

In this echo chamber, I run wild,
Like a child in the candy aisle,
Hilarious echoes spinning about,
With each laugh, there's nothing to doubt!

Reverb of comedy fills the air,
With every giggle, I shed despair.
Inner caverns where joy plays a role,
In this reverb, I find my soul!

Paths We Never Walked

In sneakers bright, we meant to stroll,
But lost our way, that's how we roll.
Each step we take, we trip and dash,
Who knew that grass could turn to ash?

We marched in line, a duck parade,
One fell in mud, the rest were swayed.
Laughter echoed, not quite refined,
Our feet are silly, but oh, so blind!

We planned a route, a fancy path,
But ended up in Tom's big bath.
We splashed and flopped with sheer delight,
Oh, walking's tough—let's take a flight!

So here we are, on routes we missed,
With grins so wide, we can't resist.
Adventure's calling, let's just go,
Despite the paths we do not know!

Cracks in the Silence

In the quietude, we made a sound,
With snorts and giggles all around.
A paper crinkled, then a sneeze,
Oh, who'd think silence would tease?

The walls they listened, quite bemused,
As we cracked jokes, they were confused.
Whispers turned into loud guffaws,
Even the curtains had some flaws!

A creaky chair joined in the fun,
It wheezed and squeaked, a perfect pun.
With every silence, a joke was sown,
In this loud laugh, we found our own!

So let them judge, the muggles frown,
In this raucous joke-telling town.
We found the cracks where silence lay,
And filled them up with joy today!

Seeds of Revelation

Planted some thoughts in garden beds,
Wondered why they bloomed with reds.
Did I just plant a silly bean,
Or did the thoughts become a scene?

With every weed, a thought did grow,
It whispered secrets, 'Pssst, hello!'
The daisies giggled, the roses sighed,
In this maze of musings, we must abide.

One sprout had dreams of being tall,
But turned out stubby—not tall at all.
"What wisdom sprouts from this delight?"
Said the pumpkin with a wink, so bright!

So here we sow, our trivial quests,
With thoughts like seeds, we never rest.
In gardens wild, where laughter thrives,
We dig for truths in our crazy lives!

Layers of Light

Beneath the glow, we found our way,
In bursting colors, night and day.
A lampshade danced—oh, what a sight,
Who knew shadows could bring such light?

We walked through prisms, slid on beams,
With giggles caught in silver streams.
Each corner turned, a rainbow chase,
Of every hue, we joined the race.

Light up the night, let troubles fade,
In shining moments, we all wade.
We cracked the codes of joy so bright,
And laughed ourselves into the night!

So layer on the laughter loud,
For in the glow, we're all so proud.
Creating sparks, igniting glee,
In mystic lights, we roam so free!

www.ingramcontent.com/pod-product-compliance
Lightning Source LLC
Chambersburg PA
CBHW051641160426
43209CB00004B/739